KATELYN SALYERS AND NATHAN L. MASSIE

THE LETTERS OF
1 & 2 THESSALONIANS

A 10-WEEK
BIBLE STUDY GUIDE

LIGHTHOUSE SERIES

1 & 2 Thessalonians: A 10-Week Bible Study Guide
Copyright © 2026 by Katelyn Salyers and Nathan L. Massie.
Series: *Lighthouse Bible Study Guides*

Soterion Press
An imprint of Spirit & Truth Fellowship International
10 South Main Street #1737
Martinsville, IN 46151
stfi.org

Printed in the United States of America

CATALOGING-IN-PUBLICATION DATA
Names: Salyers, Katelyn, 2000—author. | Massie, Nathan L., 1995—author. |
     Wierwille, Jeremiah J. E., 1984 —editor.
Title: 1 & 2 Thessalonians: A 10-Week Bible Study Guide / Katelyn Salyers and
     Nathan L. Massie.
Description: Martinsville: Soterion Press, an imprint Spirit & Truth Fellowship
     International [2026]
Identifiers: LCCN 2025928142 | ISBN 979-8-218-71026-2 (paperback) | ISBN
     978-1-970908-99-2 (ebook)
Subjects: LCSH: Bible.—New Testament. | Bible.—Epistles of Paul. | Bible.—Thessa-
     lonians—Study and teaching.
Classification: DDC 227.81/07—dc23/eng/20260116
LC record available at: https://lccn.loc.gov/2025928142

The views expressed are those of the author and the author alone and do not necessarily reflect the official policy or position of the publisher. Any references to real persons are used with permission or are drawn from publicly available sources. But where necessary, certain names or identifying details have been altered or changed to protect privacy and anonymity.

Edited by Jeremiah Wierwille and Renee Dugan
Cover design by Sujay Paul
Interior design by Katelyn Salyers

CONTENTS

Series Preface i

How To Use This Guide iii

The Letters of 1 & 2 Thessalonians 1

Maps 17

1 Thessalonians Introduction 19

Study 1 | 1:1–10 21

Study 2 | 2:1–20 31

Study 3 | 3:1–13 41

Study 4 | 4:1–12 51

Study 5 | 4:13–5:7 59

Study 6 | 5:8–28 67

2 Thessalonians Introduction 77

Study 7 | 1:1–12 81

Study 8 | 2:1–12 89

Study 9 | 2:13–3:5 97

Study 10 | 3:6–18 105

Resources For Further Study 113

About the Authors 115

The Revised English Version 117

SERIES PREFACE

LIGHTHOUSE BIBLE STUDY GUIDES is a series that was created to help readers learn more about the light and truth of God's message in Scripture. Each volume focuses on one (or more) book(s) of the Bible and is divided into multiple studies (usually between 6-12 studies), depending upon the length of the Bible book(s) included in the volume.

The structure of each study is designed in such a way as to be useful for either individual study or group discussion. Regarding individual study, the Introduction and Scripture passage can be read and the questions contemplated at a self-directed pace and as their time permits. For group study format, the Introductions and Study Questions are intended to promote fruitful engagement with the scriptural text and enriching dialogue around its meaning and significance in the life of the believer as a follower of Christ.

Following each Study Question, space is provided for writing an answer to the prompt, personal notes, or even additional ideas for consideration as they relate to the study question. Also, it allows for reflection on the personal and practical implications of the prompt and the related verses in the passage.

Each study also contains "Supplemental Material" with Word Definitions of important terms and Additional

Notes on selected aspects of the Bible passage that will help the reader deepen their understanding.

Lastly, the Bible translation used is the Revised English Version (REV). The REV can be accessed online at revbible.com or through the "REV Bible" app on Android or Apple devices. While it is not necessary to use the REV translation exclusively, the quoted scriptures and many of the insights conveyed in the Additional Notes relate directly to the REV text. Thus, even though the reader would likely benefit more from using the REV, the reader can also use any Bible version of their choosing and still greatly benefit from the study guide. Nevertheless, the REV text is provided at the beginning of the guide for the reader's convenience.

In order to get the most out of this study guide, it is recommended to read the highlighted Bible passage that is relevant to each study before proceeding to the Introduction and the Study Questions.

May God illuminate the eyes of your understanding so that you may know the life-giving message of truth that He has given to us through the light of His Word.

Jeremiah J. E. Wierwille
Albany, 2026

HOW TO USE THIS GUIDE

WELCOME to *Lighthouse Bible Study Guides*! Whether you are exploring God's Word for the first time or are a seasoned student of Scripture, these guides are designed to help you dig deeper, ask meaningful questions, and apply biblical truth to your daily life. The purpose of this study is not only to grow your knowledge of the Bible but also to draw you closer to God and encourage a vibrant, personal relationship with Him through His Son Jesus Christ.

Each study in this guide covers a specific passage of Scripture with thought-provoking questions, space for reflection, and opportunities to engage with what you've read. The guide is flexible—structured enough to be specific and focused, but yet open-ended enough to allow God's spirit to lead you and teach you in unexpected ways.

Whether you are going to be studying by yourself or with a group, you will grow and learn more about God's grace-filled, life-giving message in Scripture through *Lighthouse Bible Study Guides*.

SUGGESTIONS FOR GROUP DISCUSSION

Studying the Bible with others brings richness and perspective that can deepen your understanding and strengthen your faith in greater ways than what you could achieve on your own. If you're using this guide with a small group, here are a few ways to make your time together the most fruitful:

1. Have a facilitator. Each session will run more smoothly with someone designated to guide the discussion and keep things on track, while encouraging everyone to share and keeping balance and peace within the group. There is a separate "Leader Guide" designed to assist the facilitator in coordinating and fostering group discussion. We encourage the facilitator to consult that volume for additional supporting material and helpful suggestions in each study.

2. Create a welcoming atmosphere. Begin each session with prayer and maybe even a few minutes of casual conversation to help get people talking. Build an environment where everyone feels safe to speak, ask questions, and share honestly. Remember, honest and respectful questions should be met with honest and respectful answers.

3. Stay focused. Try to stay centered on the Scripture passage and the questions provided in the guide, while also allowing space for God's spirit to lead the discussion in meaningful and unplanned directions. Don't control the discussion so much that it begins to stifle people's enthusiasm and interest in participating.

4. Listen well. Practice active listening. Value the different perspectives in your group—sometimes the greatest insight comes from hearing how others have encountered God or the Lord Jesus through Scripture or have come to more fully understand its meaning. No one has all the answers, and you might be surprised at what you can learn by listening to others.

5. Be respectful of time. Be mindful of time so the conversation remains focused and everyone has a chance to contribute. If some want to linger and discuss more afterward, that's great! Encourage continued conversation after the session for those lively discussions that need to be paused in order to move on in the study.

6. Pray together. Close each session with prayer, lifting up personal requests, giving thanks to God, and asking for wisdom to apply the light of God's Word through what has been learned.

SUGGESTIONS FOR INDIVIDUAL STUDY

Studying the Bible on your own can be one of the most rewarding spiritual practices. Here are some tips for getting the most out of your personal study time with this guide:

1. Set a consistent schedule. Choose a regular time and place where you can be quiet, focused, and free from distractions. Whether it's in the morning with a cup of coffee or in the evening before bed, consistency will help form a meaningful habit.

2. Begin with prayer. Before studying, first ask God to open your heart and mind to understand His Word.

Invite God to enlighten the understanding of your mind and speak to you through the Scriptures.

3. Read slowly and reflectively. Don't rush through the studies. Learning is best achieved by slow and intentional deliberation. You don't have to reflect and answer every single question in the guide, but by taking time to carefully consider what the question is asking rather than breezing through them, you will gain a greater understanding of the Bible and its significance for your life. In other words, use the study questions to help you reflect deeply on the meaning and application of Scripture.

4. Take notes. In addition to reflecting on Scripture, it can help to write down your thoughts, prayers, and any insights you gain. Keeping a journal of your study as you go through the guide can help you track your spiritual growth and understanding over time. It can also enable you to revisit certain unanswered questions for further study after completing the guide.

5. Be honest. Don't be afraid to wrestle with difficult questions or admit when you don't understand something in the Bible. The process of seeking and asking is part of the journey. Everyone starts some place, but the key is to be hungry and to continue seeking deeper knowledge and understanding of God and His message in Scripture.

6. Memorize a verse. Consider choosing one verse from each session to memorize or meditate on during the week. Write this verse down somewhere convenient so that you can read and recite it throughout the week.

WORD OF ENCOURAGEMENT

As you begin this journey through the Scriptures, remember this: God delights in revealing Himself to those who seek Him. God's Word is alive and powerful—it has the potential to transform your heart, renew your mind, and equip you for every good work. Whether you're studying alone or gathered with friends and acquaintances, trust that God is at work in you as you faithfully pursue Him. Be patient with the process, stay open to receive what God's spirit reveals to you, and don't forget to enjoy the journey. God has something special in store for you in the weeks ahead. Let God's light guide your path as you devote yourself to studying His Word!

"Your word is a lamp to my feet, yes, a light for my path."

~Psalm 119:105 (REV)

THE FIRST LETTER TO THE THESSALONIANS

CHAPTER 1

OPENING GREETING (1:1-10)
Salutation

[1]Paul, and Silvanus,[a] and Timothy, to the church of the Thessalonians *who are* in *union with* God the Father and the Lord Jesus Christ:[b] Grace to you and peace.

Prayer

[2]We give thanks to God always for all of you, constantly remembering *you* in our prayers, [3]remembering before our God and Father your work motivated by trust, and labor prompted by love, and endurance based on hope in our Lord Jesus Christ.

Imitators and Examples

[4]For we know, brothers and sisters who are loved by God, that you were chosen, [5]because our good news did not come to you in word only, but also in power, and in the holy spirit, and with much assurance. You know the kind of people we were among you for your sake. [6]And you became imitators of us and of the Lord when you received the word with joy from the holy spirit, in *spite of* much affliction. [7]As a result, you became an example to all those who believe in Macedonia and in Achaia. [8]For the word of the Lord has sounded forth from you, not

---

[a] Or "Silas"

[b] Lit. "the Anointed One"

only in Macedonia and Achaia, but your trust toward God has gone out into every place, so that we do not need to say anything, ⁹because they themselves are reporting about us, how we *conducted ourselves when we* came to you,[c] and how you turned to God from idols to serve a living and true God ¹⁰and to wait for his Son from heaven, whom he raised out from the dead—Jesus—the one who rescues us from the wrath to come.

CHAPTER 2

PAUL'S MINISTRY (2:1-19)
Paul's Conduct

¹For you yourselves know, brothers and sisters, that our coming[d] to you was not in vain. ²On the contrary, after having suffered and having been shamefully mistreated at Philippi, as you know, we were bold because of our *trust in* God[e] to speak to you the good news of God in spite of much opposition. ³For our appeal did not come from error or from impure motives, nor *was it made* in deceit, ⁴but since we have been approved by God to be entrusted with the good news, therefore we speak it, not to please people, but *to please* God, who is testing our hearts.

⁵For we never used flattering speech, as you know, nor had greed as a motive (God is *our* witness), ⁶nor were we seeking glory from people, neither from you nor from others, although we could have made demands as apos-

---

[c] Or "how we were welcomed among you"
[d] Lit. "entrance"
[e] Lit. "we were bold in our God"

tles of Christ,[f] [7]instead, we were *like* infants *when we were* among you. We were like a nursing mother tenderly caring for her own children, [8]having such great affection for you that we were pleased to share with you not only the good news of God but also our own souls, because you had become deeply loved by us. [9]For you remember, brothers and sisters, our labor and struggles; working night and day so that we would not be a burden to any of you, we preached to you the good news of God. [10]You are witnesses, and God *also*, of how purely and righteously and blamelessly we behaved toward you who believe. [11]As you know, we *treated* each one of you as a father *treats* his own children, [12]encouraging you and comforting you and urging you so that you walk in a manner worthy of God, who calls you into his own kingdom and glory.

Receiving the Word of God

[13]And we also constantly thank God for this: that when you received the word of God that you heard from us, you accepted it not as the word of men, but as it truly is, the word of God, which is at work in you who believe. [14]For you, brothers and sisters, became imitators of the churches of God in Judea that are in Christ Jesus, because you also suffered the same things from your own countrymen as they did from the Jews, [15]who killed both the Lord Jesus and the prophets and drove us out and do not please God and are hostile to all people [16]by hindering us from speaking to the Gentiles so that they can be saved. As a result, they are continuing to pile up their sins, but the wrath *of God* has come upon them until the end.

---

[f] Lit. "the Anointed One"

Desire to Visit

¹⁷But we, brothers and sisters, after being orphaned from you for a period of time (in person,[g] not in heart), were all the more eager to see your face—we greatly desired it.[h] ¹⁸For we wanted to come to you (even I, Paul, *attempted to* again and again), but the Adversary[i] prevented us. ¹⁹For who is our hope or joy or crown of boasting in the presence of our Lord Jesus at his coming? Is it not you? ²⁰For you are our glory and joy.

CHAPTER 3

TIMOTHY'S REPORT (3:1-13)
Sending Timothy

¹Therefore, when we could bear it no longer, we thought it best to stay behind in Athens by ourselves, ²and we sent Timothy, our brother and fellow worker for God in *spreading* the good news of Christ,[j] to strengthen and encourage you concerning your trust, ³so that no one is shaken by these afflictions, because you know that we are destined for this. ⁴For even when we were with you, we kept telling you in advance that we were going to suffer affliction, and as you know, it came to pass. ⁵For this reason, when I could bear it no longer, I sent *Timothy* to find out about your trust, because I was afraid that somehow the Tempter had tempted you and our labor would have been in vain.

---

[g] Lit. "face"
[h] Lit. "with great desire"
[i] "Adversary" is the translation of the Greek *satanas*.
[j] Lit. "the Anointed One"

An Encouraging Report

[6]But Timothy has just now come to us from you and has brought us good news about your trust and love, and that you always remember us with affection, longing to see us, just as we also *long to see* you. [7]Because of this, brothers and sisters, in all our distress and affliction we have been encouraged about you because of your trust. [8]For now we *really* live, since you are standing firm in the Lord. [9]For how can we give thanks to God for you in return for all of our joy and rejoicing[k] before our God because of you? [10]Night and day we keep praying most earnestly for *an opportunity* to see your face and to supply what is lacking in your trust.

Prayer for Growth

[11]Now may our God and Father himself and our Lord Jesus guide our way to you, [12]and may the Lord cause you to increase and overflow in love for one another and for all people, just as we also do for you, [13]so that your hearts will be strengthened *so that you will be* blameless in *your* holiness before our God and Father at the coming of our Lord Jesus with all his holy ones.

CHAPTER 4

LIVING HOLY LIVES (4:1-12)
Walking in Holiness

[1]Furthermore then, brothers and sisters, we ask and encourage you in the Lord Jesus, that just as you learned from us how you must walk and please God—indeed,

---

[k] Lit. "the joy with which we rejoice"

you are *already* walking in this way—that you would do so even more. [2]For you know what commands we gave you by *the authority of* the Lord Jesus. [3]For this is the will of God—for you to be holy: *that is*, that you abstain from sexual immorality; [4]that each one of you know how to control his own vessel in holiness and honor, [5]not in lustful passion like the Gentiles who do not know God; [6]*and* that no one overstep proper boundaries and take advantage of his brother or sister in this matter, because the Lord is an avenger of all these *offenses*, just as we told you before and solemnly warned you. [7]For God did not call us to be impure, but *to live* in holiness. [8]Therefore, the one who rejects *these commands* does not reject a human being but God, who gives his holy spirit to you.

Love and Proper Conduct

[9]Now concerning affection for *God's* family, you do not need *anyone* to write to you because you yourselves are taught by God to love one another. [10]For indeed, that is what you are doing for all the brothers and sisters in the whole *region* of Macedonia. And we encourage you, brothers and sisters, to do so even more, [11]and to make it your aim to lead a peaceable life,[1] and to attend to your own business, and to work with your hands, just as we commanded you, [12]so that you walk properly toward outsiders, and so that you do not need anything.

The Hope of Christ's Return

[13]Now we do not want you to be ignorant, brothers and sisters, concerning those who are asleep, so that you do not grieve like the rest *of humankind,* who have no hope. [14]For since we believe that Jesus died and was raised, so

---

[1] Or "quiet life."

also *we believe that* through Jesus, God will bring *to life* those who have fallen asleep *so that they will be* with him.[m] [15]For this we say to you by the word of the Lord, that we who are alive, who are left until the coming of the Lord, will certainly not precede those who have fallen asleep. [16]For the Lord himself will descend from heaven with a loud command, with the voice of a ruling angel, and with *the sound of* the trumpet of God, and the dead in Christ[n] will rise first. [17]Then we who are alive, who are left, will be suddenly caught up together with them in the clouds, for a meeting with the Lord in the air, and so we will always be with the Lord. [18]So then, comfort one another with these words.

CHAPTER 5

THE DAY OF THE LORD (5:1-11)
Children of Light

[1]Now concerning the times and dates, brothers and sisters, you do not need anything to be written to you [2]because you yourselves know very well that the Day of the Lord will come like a thief in the night. [3]When they are saying, "Peace and safety!" then disaster will suddenly come upon them like labor pains upon a pregnant woman, and they will surely not escape. [4]But you, brothers and sisters, are not in darkness that the Day would surprise you like a thief, [5]because you are all children of light and children of the day. We are not of the night, nor of

---

[m] Or "so also *we believe that* through Jesus, God will bring *to life*, in addition to him, those who have fallen asleep."
[n] Lit. "the Anointed One"

the darkness. ⁶So then, let us not be asleep like the rest *of humankind,* but let us be awake and clearheaded. ⁷For those who sleep, sleep at night, and those who get drunk, get drunk at night.

Faith, Love, and Hope

⁸But since we are of the day, let us be clearheaded, putting on a breastplate of trust and love, and as a helmet, the hope of salvation. ⁹For God did not appoint us to wrath, but to obtain salvation through our Lord Jesus Christ, ¹⁰who died in our place so that whether we are awake or asleep, we will live together with him. ¹¹ "Therefore encourage one another and build each other up, just as you are already doing.

ADDITIONAL INSTRUCTIONS (5:12-22)
Honor Church Leaders

¹²Now, brothers and sisters, we request that you respect those who labor among you and are leading[o] you in the Lord and are admonishing[p] you, ¹³and to hold them in very high regard with love because of their work. Be at peace among yourselves.

Exhortations

¹⁴Now we urge you, brothers and sisters, admonish[q] the undisciplined, comfort the discouraged, help the weak, be patient with everyone. ¹⁵See to it that no one repays anyone evil for evil, but always diligently pursue what is good for one another and for all people.

---

[o] Or "caring for"
[p] Or "counseling"
[q] Or "counsel"

¹⁶Rejoice always; ¹⁷never stop praying; ¹⁸in everything give thanks, for this is the will of God for you in Christ Jesus.

¹⁹Do not quench[r] the spirit. ²⁰Do not treat prophecies with contempt, ²¹but test everything *and* hold on firmly to what is good. ²²Stay away from every kind of evil.

FINAL REMARKS (5:23-28)
Prayer
²³Now may the God of peace himself make you completely holy, and may your whole spirit and soul and body be preserved without blame at the coming of our Lord Jesus Christ. ²⁴The one who calls you is faithful, and he will do this.

Farewell Greetings
²⁵Brothers and sisters, pray for us. ²⁶Greet all the brothers and sisters with a holy kiss. ²⁷I put you under oath before the Lord that this letter be read to all the brothers and sisters. ²⁸The grace of our Lord Jesus Christ[s] be with you all.

---

[r] Or "suppress"
[s] Lit. "the Anointed One"

THE SECOND LETTER TO THE THESSALONIANS

CHAPTER 1

OPENING GREETING (1:1-4)
Salutation

[1]Paul, and Silvanus,[a] and Timothy, to the church of the Thessalonians *who are* in *union with* God our Father and the Lord Jesus Christ:[b] [2]Grace to you and peace from God our Father and the Lord Jesus Christ.

Prayer

[3]We are obligated to always give thanks to God for all of you, brothers and sisters, and rightly so, because your trust is growing abundantly, and the love each one of you all has for one another is increasing. [4]Therefore, we ourselves boast about you in the churches of God because of your endurance and trust in *the midst of* all your persecutions and afflictions that you are enduring.

GOD'S RIGHTEOUS JUDGMENT (1:5-12)
Encouragement in Persecution

[5]*The fact* that you will be counted worthy of the kingdom of God (for which you also are suffering) is evidence of the righteous judgment of God, [6]since it is righteous for God to repay with affliction those who are afflicting you [7]and *to give* relief to you who are being afflicted, as well as to us, when the Lord Jesus is revealed from heaven with

---

[a] Or "Silas"
[b] Lit. "the Anointed One"

his powerful angels [8]in flaming fire taking vengeance on those who do not know God and on those who do not obey the good news of our Lord Jesus. [9]They will pay the penalty of everlasting destruction away from the presence of the Lord and away from his glorious strength[c] [10]on that Day when he comes to be glorified by his holy ones and to be marveled at by all those who believed (*this includes you* because our testimony to you was believed).

Worthy of His Calling

[11]And in view of this we always pray for you, that our God will count you worthy of *his* calling and by *his* power fulfill every desire for goodness and *every* work motivated by trust, [12]so that the name of our Lord Jesus will be glorified in you, and you in him, according to the grace of our God and the Lord Jesus Christ.

CHAPTER 2

THE COMING OF CHRIST (2:1-12)
Man of Lawlessness

[1]Now concerning the coming of our Lord Jesus Christ[d] and our gathering together to him, we ask you, brothers and sisters, [2]not to be quickly shaken from your *state of* mind or alarmed, either by a spirit-*inspired utterance* or by a *spoken* message or by a letter allegedly from us, to the effect that the Day of the Lord has come. [3]Do not let anyone deceive you by any means, because *that day will not come* unless the apostasy comes first and the man of lawlessness

---

[c] Lit. "the glory of his strength"

[d] Lit. "the Anointed One"

is revealed, the son of destruction, [4]who opposes and exalts himself above every so-called "god" or *every* object of worship, so much so that he sits down in the sanctuary of God, displaying himself as God. [5]Do you not remember that when I was still with you I told you these things? [6]And you know what is holding *him* back now, so that he will be revealed when his time comes. [7]For the secret of lawlessness is already at work only until the one who is now restraining *it* is out of the way. [8]And then the lawless one will be revealed, whom the Lord Jesus will destroy by the spirit[e] from his mouth and put an end *to him* at the appearance of his coming.

Activity of the Adversary

[9]The coming *of the lawless one* is a result of the activity of the Adversary[f] with all kinds of power and counterfeit signs and wonders, [10]and with every kind of unrighteous deception to *deceive* those who are destroying themselves because they refused to love the truth and so be saved. [11]And because of this God sends them a deluding influence[g] so that they believe a lie, [12]with the result that all who have not believed the truth, but took pleasure in unrighteousness, will be condemned.

CALL TO STAND FIRM (2:13-17)

Exhortation

[13]But we are obligated to give thanks to God always for you, brothers and sisters loved by the Lord, because God chose you as the firstfruits[h] for salvation *that comes*

---

[e] Or "breath"

[f] "Adversary" is the translation of the Greek *satanas*.

[g] Lit. "working of error"

[h] Some MSS read "from the beginning"

through holiness produced by the spirit and belief in the truth. ¹⁴He called you to this through our good news, so you can obtain the glory of our Lord Jesus Christ.

Prayer

¹⁵So then, brothers and sisters, stand firm and hold on to the traditions that you were taught, whether by *spoken* message or letter from us. ¹⁶Now may our Lord Jesus Christ himself and God our Father, who loved us and by *his* grace gave us everlasting encouragement and a good hope, ¹⁷encourage and strengthen your hearts in every good work and word.

CHAPTER 3

PRAYER REQUEST AND WARNING (3:1-15)
Pray for us

¹Furthermore, brothers and sisters, keep praying for us so that the word of the Lord continues to spread *quickly* and be glorified, just as it also did among you, ²and *pray* so that we are rescued from harmful and wicked people, for not everyone has trust. ³But the Lord is faithful, who will strengthen you and guard you from the Wicked One. ⁴And we have confidence concerning you *who are* in the Lord, that you are both doing and will *continue to* do the things that we command. ⁵Now may the Lord guide your hearts into the love of God and into the endurance of Christ.ⁱ

ⁱ Lit. "the Anointed One"

Warning Against the Disorderly

⁶Now we command you, brothers and sisters, in the name of our Lord Jesus Christ, that you keep away from every brother or sister who walks disorderly and not according to the tradition that they received from us. ⁷For you yourselves know how you must imitate us, because we were not disorderly among you, ⁸nor did we eat bread from anyone without paying *for it*. Instead, we labored and struggled, working night and day so that we would not be a burden to any of you, ⁹not because we do not have the right *to be supported*, but so that we could give ourselves to you as an example for you to imitate. ¹⁰And indeed, when we were with you, we used to give you this command: "If anyone is not willing to work, do not let him eat." ¹¹For we hear that some among you are walking disorderly, not *busy* working, but are *just* busybodies. ¹²Now we command and exhort such people in the *name of the* Lord Jesus Christ to be working in a quiet fashion *and* to eat their own bread.

¹³But as for you, brothers and sisters, do not grow weary in doing what is good. ¹⁴But if anyone does not obey our instruction in this letter, take note of that person *and* do not associate with him, so that he is put to shame. ¹⁵And *yet* do not regard him as an enemy, but admonishʲ him as a brother or sister.

FINAL REMARKS (3:16-18)

¹⁶Now may the Lord of peace himself give you peace at all times *and* in every way. The Lord be with you all.

ʲ Or "counsel"

¹⁷I, Paul, write this greeting with my own hand, which is the sign *of genuineness* in every letter; this is how I write. ¹⁸The grace of our Lord Jesus Christ be with you all.

Adriatic Sea
Black Sea
ITALIA
MACEDONIA
THRACE
PONTUS
BITHYNIA
Tyrrhenus Sea
Samothrace
MYSIA
ASIA MINOR
GALATIA
CAPPADOCIA
Aegean Sea
Lesbos
ACHAIA
PISIDIA
PHRYGIA
LYCAONIA
SICILY
Ionian Sea
Chios
Samos
CILICIA
Cos
PAMPHYLIA
LYCIA
MALTA
CRETE
SYRIA
CYPRUS
MEDITERRANEAN SEA
JUDEA
ARABIA
EGYPT

MACEDONIA
THRACE
Philippi
Amphipolis
Neapolis
Thessalonica
Berea
Apollonia
Samothrace
Troas
MYSIA
Assos
Lesbos
Mitylene
Pergamum
Thyatira
Aegean Sea
ACHAIA

1 THESSALONIANS INTRODUCTION

First Thessalonians is an ancient letter, written by the Apostle Paul alongside his companions Silvanus and Timothy (1:1). Paul introduces himself as a devoted servant of the good news, encouraging the Thessalonians to "walk in a manner worthy of God" (2:9–12). He acknowledges the hardships he and his companions faced, including opposition from the Philippians (2:2) and Athenians (3:1–4).

Addressing the Gentile congregations in the city of Thessalonica in Asia Minor (1:1), Paul praises their unwavering hope in Jesus and their commitment to the good news (1:2). He commends them for becoming "imitators of the apostles and the Lord" (1:6), enduring suffering with joy (1:6). Their patient endurance—especially in the face of adversity—sets them apart from the Jewish community Paul references as a distinct group (2:14).

Paul's tone throughout the letter is kind and personal, likening himself to a "father with his children" (2:11) and seeing the Thessalonians as his spiritual children in Christ. He expresses a deep desire to visit them again (2:17) and writes as an overseer, genuinely concerned for their spiritual growth and eager to strengthen their faith (3:2). Paul's relationship with the Thessalonians is multifaceted, but each facet serves to nurture their trust in the Lord Jesus.

Paul also addresses theological questions, particularly concerning those who have died before Jesus' return (4:13). He reassures the Thessalonians, asserting the truth and expressing his desire that they not be uninformed about the resurrection and what will happen to those who have died believing in Jesus (4:13–14). The resurrection serves as both a first-century and present-day hope for believers—Jesus will raise those who have died in Him to life. Those who die before His return are not at a disadvantage, but instead hold a place of honor on that resurrection day—rising first to escort King Jesus to the earth in a glorious, triumphant, and imperial entry.

Paul's letter is brimming with encouragement, urging them to keep growing in their trust in the Lord by promoting the good news of Jesus Christ and living exemplary lives before those outside the church. He offers practical guidance for spiritual growth—praying continually, rejoicing always, abstaining from idolatry, and pursuing what is good (5:14–22)—all with the aim of strengthening the churches in Thessalonica's faith in Jesus Christ and the hope of the resurrection in the coming age.

STUDY 1

INTRODUCTION

The churches in Thessalonica were planted by Paul during his second missionary journey, but he and his companions (including Silvanus and Timothy) were forced to leave when some local Jews opposed the message of the good news (cf. Acts 17:1-9). Despite this, Paul remained deeply connected to the Thessalonians. In his letter, he warmly greets them with "grace and peace," a familiar and meaningful opening Paul often used to greet believers.

From the start, Paul's love for them is clear. He tells them that he regularly prays for them, showing both his care and offering an example they can follow. Paul acknowledges that the Thessalonians aren't just passively accepting the good news. Instead, they are actively working for it, not out of fear or for personal gain, but because of their trust in God. Their work, Paul says, is driven by faith (1 Thess. 1:3a).

Paul also recognizes the suffering they've endured for the sake of the good news. The Thessalonians have faced persecution, and he empathizes with their struggles. But Paul encourages them to persevere, pointing out that their endurance is rooted in hope—hope in Jesus Christ (1 Thess. 1:3c). Even in the face of pressure, they've held firm to their faith. In the first century, persecution often caused people to turn away from their faith. But the Thessalonians have shown remarkable strength by standing firm in the faith despite facing opposition and hostility.

They've turned away from idols—a huge deal in their culture—and committed themselves to following the true God. In a world where idol worship was the norm, their decision to forsake all other gods was not only counter-cultural, but downright courageous. Paul wraps up this opening section by emphasizing that turning from idols to the one true God brings with it a promise: rescue from the wrath that will come when Christ returns. Through their faith and endurance, the Thessalonians are secure in the hope of salvation, both now and in the future.

STUDY QUESTIONS

1 After his opening greeting, how does Paul express his attitude toward the Thessalonians, and what tone does it set for the letter? [1 Thess. 1:1-2a]

2 In what way might Paul's practice of prayer be a model for our own prayers? [1 Thess. 1:2b]

3 Paul mentions three virtues of the Thessalonians: their "work motivated by trust," "labor prompted by love," and "endurance based on hope in our Lord Jesus Christ" (v. 3). Have you seen these virtues, either in your life, or those around you? If so, how did you observe them being lived out? [1 Thess. 1:3]

4 Paul tells the Thessalonians that they are loved and chosen by God because they received the good news: "in word," "in power," "in the holy spirit," and "with much assurance" (v. 5). Share how you see one (or more) of these phrases being connected to the good news. [1 Thess. 1:4-5]

5 How did you respond when you first heard the good news?

6 Paul says that the Thessalonians became "imitators of the Lord". What are some of the practical aspects of the Lord's example that can be challenging to imitate? [1 Thess. 1:6]

7 Paul commends the Thessalonians for their example of trusting the good news and how their reputation is known throughout the whole region. Is there an example of a believer's life, whether you know them personally or not, that you find inspiring? How has your spiritual life been impacted by witnessing their dedication to the Lord? [1 Thess. 1:7]

8 What's an example of a modern "idol" in our culture that people have a hard time "turning from"? [1 Thess. 1:9]

9 Reports were being spread about the way Paul and his companions conducted themselves among the Thessalonians. In the biblical culture, how do you think their behavior affected the Thessalonians' willingness to hear the good news? [1 Thess. 1:9-10]

10 How does waiting for Jesus' return affect the way you live? [1 Thess. 1:10]

WORD DEFINITIONS

GOOD NEWS [v. 5]

The Greek word *euangelion* is often translated as "gospel;" the word "gospel" is an old English word that means "good story." But it does not refer to a fictional story, but a story about what has happened, and thus, it means "good news." This "good news" is about Jesus—God's Anointed One—who fulfilled all the Old Testament messianic prophecies, established a new covenant, inaugurated the coming of God's kingdom, and has brought about the beginning of new creation and the promised restoration of all things.

HOLY SPIRIT [v. 5]

The holy spirit is the power and the presence of God. Born-again believers receive the holy spirit as a gift from God that empowers them to live holy lives, develop godly virtues, and demonstrate the power of the spirit through various spiritual gifts.

MACEDONIA [v. 7]

A Roman territory in northern Greece with the capital of Thessalonica. Paul established a relationship with the Macedonians by traveling across the Aegean Sea during his second missionary journey (cf. Acts 16:11-17:15)

ACHAIA [v. 7]

A Roman territory in southern Greece whose most prominent city was Corinth. Paul visited this region during his second missionary journey.

IDOLATRY / IDOLS [v. 9]

Any religious practices or forms of worship outside of the Jewish monotheistic faith, often involving icons or statues that represent false gods. Pagan idol worship varied from culture to culture, but all idolatry ultimately steals the reverence and recognition that is rightly due to the one true God–Yahweh.

HEAVEN [v. 10]

Refers to the realm where God dwells with His angelic armies and the divine council around his throne. It can also refer to the sky where birds fly, and even the farthest reaches of outer space.

WRATH TO COME [v. 10]

A phrase that refers to "the day of the Lord" — a time in the age to come when God will bring justice to the whole world by punishing the wicked, vanquishing evil, and establishing His righteous rule. God's "wrath" is His righteous indignation toward sin and those who disobey Him and oppose His authority.

ADDITIONAL NOTES

"chosen" [v. 4]

The word "chosen" does not inherently carry the idea of "chosen to be saved" (or not to be saved) or "chosen" in a predestined sense. The language of being "chosen" carries a variety of meanings throughout the Scriptures. For example, believers are "chosen" to receive a resurrected body like Jesus (Rom. 8:29), Jesus "chose" twelve disciples (Luke 6:13), God "chose" Israel as a People (Acts 13:17), Jesus "chose" Paul to carry his name as a witness (Acts 9:15), and God has "chosen" those in Christ before the foundation of the world (Eph 1:4). Thus, when the word "chosen" occurs, the context determines the meaning for who was chosen and what they were chosen for, or chosen to receive. Importantly, many occurrences of "chosen" in both the Old and New Testaments speak about God choosing various individuals and groups as part of His plans and purposes. But being "chosen" doesn't negate the capacity of human free will for the agent that is chosen to embrace or reject God's choice of them. Often, being "chosen" entails a positive response on the part of the individual to God's calling or invitation. Therefore, "choosing" God becomes one of the ways/reasons that a person is said to be "chosen" in Scripture (like the Thessalonians).

"good news" [v. 5]

The good news (often called "the gospel") is the announcement that life in the age to come is available to all who place their trust in Jesus—through his death and resurrection. At the start of his public ministry (Luke 4), Jesus quotes Isaiah 61:1, identifying himself as the one who would bring this restoration through the good news he proclaims. He boldly affirms that he is the very figure referred to by the Lord Yahweh in Isaiah 61:1. In the first century, the term "good news" also had a secular meaning. The emperor's "good news" would be announced throughout the Roman Empire, often having to do with the conquest of new land or other important news that he would want shared with all the residents of the empire.

"raised out from the dead" [v. 10]

The resurrection is the moment when God raised Jesus from the dead on the third day following his brutal crucifixion. What makes Jesus' resurrection unique is that he was raised to immortality, never to die again—unlike Lazarus, who was brought back to life only to face death once more, as seen in John 11. Jesus' resurrection confirms his identity as the Son of God, uniquely commissioned to accomplish a mission only he could fulfill. By raising Jesus from the dead, God affirmed the truth and power of his teachings, but also set before us hope. Because God raised Jesus in this way, we can take hold to his promises that He will one day raise us to immortality as well.

STUDY 2

INTRODUCTION

Paul opens this part of his letter with a serious tone, reminding the Thessalonians that his visit to them was worthwhile, even though he had faced significant opposition and hardship in Philippi just before. Hardship in his missionary journeys was common to Paul. He regularly faced opposition from Jewish and Gentile communities. Recently, Paul had faced persecution from the Philippians after casting out a spirit of divination from a slave girl whose fortune telling brought her masters great profit (Acts 16:16-24). This act leads to Paul and Silas being imprisoned, but the work of the good news continues as they, in turn, convert their jail keeper (Acts 16:30-34). Paul and Silas also reach out to the Philippian Jewish community, reasoning with them about Jesus as the Messiah. However, driven by anger and jealousy, the Jews provoke a riot, driving them out of the city. (Acts

17:1-9). These examples of Paul's steadfastness prove his unyielding devotion to advancing the good news, no matter the cost.

When Paul addresses the Thessalonians, he speaks to them plainly, but confidently. He doesn't resort to flattering words to win them over, nor does he use his authority as an apostle to command their loyalty. Instead, he approaches them as a father would his own children, with firmness but parental care. Along the way, rumors had begun to spread, likely stirred up by those who opposed him and the good news, accusing him of insincere motives in his ministry. Paul urges the Thessalonians to remember their own experience with him, recalling the way he treated them and encouraging them not to be swayed by these false stories. Though his absence from them is caused by both imprisonment and spiritual opposition, Paul's deepest longing, he assures them, is to be reunited with his beloved "children" in Thessalonica.

STUDY QUESTIONS

1 After being confronted with much opposition during their last visit, Paul reminds the Thessalonians of his conduct among them. What did Paul and his fellow evangelists deliberately avoid, and what practices did they embrace while sharing the good news? [1 Thess. 2:1-6]

2 Paul mentions that they spoke not to please people, but to please God. What are some ways that we can live our lives for God rather than for people? [1 Thess. 2:4]

3 Paul says that he could have "made demands as apostles" when they were instructing the Thessalonians, but he didn't. Why do you think that Paul makes this point? [1 Thess. 2:6]

4 Why do you think Paul repeatedly emphasizes his behavior (purity, righteousness, blamelessness, etc.) toward the Thessalonians? What reason would Paul have to boast about it? [1 Thess. 2:10-12]

5 Paul says that he treated the Thessalonians like a father with his own children. What are three actions listed that explain how he interacted with the believers, and how can we apply these principles in our relationships, especially with other believers? [1 Thess. 2:11-12]

6 When the Thessalonians received the "word of God" (i.e., the good news), they accepted it not as human words but as a message truly from God. How do you personally perceive Paul's message? Why is it important to regard the good news as actually a message from God, and not as something from the human imagination? [1 Thess. 2:13]

7 How did persecution from the Jews (and also the Gentiles) affect the ministry of Paul and the Thessalonians? [Acts 17:1-15, 1 Thess. 2:14-15]

8 What's the importance of meeting together with other believers? What are the advantages or disadvantages of meeting in-person, online, or on the phone? [1 Thess. 2:17]

9 Why does Paul call the Thessalonians his "hope or joy or crown of boasting"? [1 Thess. 2:19]

10 What are some practical ways that you can encourage other believers in your life this week with your words or actions?

WORD DEFINITIONS

PHILIPPI [v. 2]

Philippi, an ancient city in northern Greece, was named after Philip II of Macedon, the father of Alexander the Great, who conquered it in 356 BC. Following the Battle of Philippi in 42 BC, the city fell under Roman rule. In the first century, Philippi's strategic location along the Via Egnatia made it a vital crossroads for the Roman Empire, fostering a hub for trade and religious interactions.

APOSTLE [v. 6]

"Apostle" is the term that is given to the disciples who were with Jesus (except for Judas Iscariot) and others in the New Testament who had seen the Lord Jesus alive before his crucifixion and after his resurrection. These are the men who are entrusted with the accurate teaching of the Christian faith, public declaration of the message of the good news, and are often involved in planting and strengthening new Christian faith communities.

KINGDOM [v. 12]

God's kingdom is the culmination of all His promises and covenants: from Abraham's descendants inheriting the earth, to the eternal throne established through David, and to the fulfillment of Christ's covenant by His blood, granting eternal life to all who believe—extending back to the saints before Him. This kingdom will be an eternal government in which evil is extinguished and justice reigns for all eternity.

GLORY [v. 12]

God's glory embodies the sum of His reputation, authority, and infinite praiseworthiness. To walk in a manner worthy of God and his glory is to live up to his expectations, faithfully representing him and his good news message.

WORD OF GOD [v. 13]

God's Word is the powerful voice of God that brings creation into existence, works miracles, and finds its ultimate expression in the good news of Jesus Christ. In this context, the "Word of God" likely refers to the "message" or "good news" of God (cf. 1 Thess. 2:2, 9), which God brought to pass through the atoning work of Jesus.

JUDEA [v .14]

To ancient Greco-Roman society, 1st-century Judea was a unique and challenging province, known for its people's unwavering devotion to one God and their distinct way of life centered on the Temple and their sacred laws. While often misunderstood and sometimes seen as troublesome, this land held deep spiritual significance as the place where God's promises to Israel were unfolding, ultimately leading to the arrival of Jesus Christ.

JEWS [v. 14]

In the first century, many Jews viewed both Gentiles and Christians as threats to their covenantal identity and traditions, often opposing their beliefs and practices to preserve the purity of their faith and way of life. This often led to Jews antagonizing Christian and Gentile communities alike.

GENTILES [v. 16]

Gentile is the term that Jews use to refer to non-Jewish pagans. In the New Testament the Gentiles are often those who are in Asia Minor and Greece, such as the non-Jewish Thessalonians.

WRATH OF GOD [v. 16]

The wrath of God reflects His ultimate and just response to sin and wicked persons, which will be fully revealed and affected when Jesus returns with the armies of heaven in the age to come.

ADVERSARY [v. 18]

The "Adversary" is a title that literally means "Slanderer." It refers to Satan, who stands as a spiritual antagonist and enemy of God, relentlessly preying on God's people with intentions to harm and destroy. However, his destructive influences in the world are only temporary in this age, as God will destroy him and his kingdom of darkness in the age to come.

ADDITIONAL NOTES

"shamefully mistreated at Philippi" [v. 2]

Paul was shamefully mistreated in Philippi during his second missionary journey, as described in Acts 16:16-24. After casting a spirit out of a slave girl who was being used by her owners for fortune telling, Paul and Silas were seized by her owners. They were accused of causing trouble in the city, brought before the magistrates, and falsely charged with promoting unlawful practices. Without a proper trial, they were stripped, beaten with rods, and thrown into prison, where they were shackled in chains. This mistreatment highlights Paul and Silas's suffering for the sake of the good news and sets the stage for the miraculous events that followed, including the conversion of the Philippian jailer.

"testing our hearts" [v. 4]

This phrase is used to reflect the examination that believers undergo as they move the good news message forward. God evaluates the true intentions and motivations behind what a person does, especially when it comes to sharing His message. For Paul, this means no longer seeking the human recognition he once pursued in his former life but focusing entirely on gaining approval from God.

"demands as apostles of Christ" [v. 6]

The apostles were entrusted with authority to issue commands in the name of the Lord Jesus. As church leaders, their words and position held significant weight, but they chose not to misuse that authority. Instead, they approached others reasonably and in humility, asking rather than demanding. So instead of insisting on deferential treatment and praise, which was certainly rightfully theirs as apostles, Paul and his companions sought true glory and honor that can only come from God.

"worthy of God" [v. 12]

Living in a manner worthy of God means leading a holy life, turning away from worldly behaviors and embracing God's authority in our lives. It involves seeking His will, maintaining moral purity, and turning to Him in repentance when we fall short.

"suffered the same things" [v. 14]

Paul compares the Thessalonians' suffering to that of the believers in Judea, who were mistreated by their religious leaders. However, while the Judean church faced opposition from their fellow citizens, the Thessalonians endured persecution from their fellow Gentiles. This highlights the dual opposition the early church faced from both Jews and Gentiles.

"until the end" [v. 16]

This continues Paul's thought from 1:10, where he explains that Jesus will come from heaven to deliver us from God's future wrath. Here, Paul refers to the unrepentant actions of the Jewish community opposing the spread of the good news. He emphasizes that God's wrath is resting upon these antagonists both now at the present time and all the way to the end of this age when Jesus returns and their due punishment will be meted out.

"the Adversary prevented us" [v. 18]

The Adversary, as God's greatest enemy and the opponent of His people, works tirelessly to deceive and disrupt, aiming to hinder the spread of the good news. In Thessalonica, the Adversary sought to isolate the believers from Paul, using persecution and social separation to weaken and divide their congregation. These same strategies are still used by the Adversary against God's people even today.

STUDY 3

INTRODUCTION

Paul's love and concern for the Thessalonians shines throughout chapter 3. He shares how difficult it was for him and his companions to be apart from them for so long. Unable to bear the separation any longer, Paul sent Timothy to check on the church and encourage them in their faith. Despite the hardships Paul and his fellow workers are enduring, he assures the Thessalonians not to be discouraged. These trials, he explains, are part of their calling as Christians, even asserting that "we are destined for this" (v. 3). For Paul, the temporary struggles of spreading the good news are completely worth it in light of the eternal impact it brings.

Paul also shares his deep concern for the Thessalonians' spiritual well-being. He admits that one of the reasons for sending Timothy to visit was for fear that the Tempter might have led them astray, as had happened with some of the other congregations Paul had established. Timothy's return to Paul, however, brought incredible news: the Thessalonians had remained faithful to the Lord, standing firm in what Paul had taught them. This fills Paul's heart with gratitude and joy, and he expresses his intense longing to see them face to face—not to verify Timothy's report, but to celebrate their shared fellowship in Christ.

In reaffirming his commitment to pray for them, Paul asks that God would continue to strengthen the Thessalonians' faith and help them remain steadfast, living blamelessly in anticipation of Jesus' return. Their faithfulness and steadfastness are not just a source of joy for Paul, but are a powerful witness to the enduring power of the good news of Jesus Christ.

STUDY QUESTIONS

1 Why were Paul, Timothy, and Silvanus so eager to visit the Thessalonians? [1 Thess. 3:1-2]

2 Paul knew that the Thessalonians were going to be persecuted. In light of this, Paul sent Timothy. What are some ways in which we can be more aware of our fellow brothers and sisters in Christ so that when they are suffering we are able to come alongside them to strengthen and encourage? [1 Thess. 3:2]

3 Imagine you were part of the Thessalonian church. How do you think you would react to Paul saying that "you were destined to suffer afflictions"? [1 Thess. 3:3]

4 How does anticipating future suffering alter your perspective on how to endure it? (cf. Rom. 5:3-5). [1 Thess. 3:3]

5 Paul seems to have been worried that the "Tempter" was attacking the Thessalonians to undo his labor among them. How does Satan leverage suffering for his plan to undermine the good news? (cf. 1 Pet. 5:8) [1 Thess. 3:5]

6 When Timothy returned to Paul, how did he describe the state of the Thessalonian church in his report? [1 Thess. 3:6]

7 What is the importance of having other believers in your life to encourage, exhort, and strengthen you in your faith? (cf. Heb. 10:23-25) [1 Thess. 3:6]

8 What does it mean to "stand firm" in the Lord? [1 Thess. 3:8]

9 Paul prays for the believers to overflow with love, which strengthens their hearts and leads to a blameless life before God at Christ's return. How does godly love shape our hearts and guide us toward holiness? (cf. 1 Pet. 4:8) [1 Thess. 3:12-13]

10 What is revealed about Paul's priorities in prayer, and how can you use his prayer to inspire and help shape your prayer life? [1 Thess. 3:10-13]

—— ◄► ——

WORD DEFINITIONS

ATHENS [v. 1]

Athens was a city in ancient Greece that once acted as the epicenter of art, philosophy, and political science. Athens, therefore, was a cultural hub where Paul delved deeply into the Gentile world to bring the good news of Jesus Christ to them. Paul visited Athens during his second missionary journey (Acts 17:16-34). Paul's original arrival in Athens was to flee the persecution he received from the Berean gentile community.

TIMOTHY [v. 2]

Timothy was a close companion of the apostle Paul, sharing a relationship akin to that of a father and son. His father was a pagan, while his mother and grandmother were Jewish. Choosing the faith of his mother, he was raised in the Jewish faith. Timothy embraced Christianity after encountering Paul, where Paul discipled Timothy and worked with him as a fellow missionary and church leader.

AFFLICTION [v. 3]

Affliction occurs when Christians receive persecution either physically from opponents of the good news message, or spiritually from Satan (the Adversary), whether directly or indirectly.

TEMPTER [v. 5]

The term "Tempter" is another name for Satan, the spiritual adversary of God, His people (i.e., believers), His kingdom, and the proclamation of the good news.

BLAMELESS [v. 13]

Blamelessness refers to the state of justification—being in a right standing and relationship with God that is granted to a person when they repent and place their faith in Jesus Christ. Yet, "blamelessness" will not be fully realized (or actually happen) until the day of judgment when believers are declared righteous and acquitted of guilt and the penalty for sin.

HOLINESS [v. 13]

Holiness is the ongoing pursuit of growing in devotion and obedience to God through repentance and turning away from sin. It is a lifelong journey that will be fully perfected when Jesus returns and God's people are resurrected.

HOLY ONES [v. 13]

In this context, "holy ones" refers to the angelic host who will be accompanying Jesus at his return. Yet, in some other places in Scripture, it refers to believers, who are "set apart" and have the holy spirit dwelling in them.

ADDITIONAL NOTES

"fellow worker for God" [v. 2]

This refers to the shared work among all believers of spreading the good news of Jesus Christ. This highlights that each of us has an equal role in the mission God has called us to. Rather than seeing one another as opponents, we should recognize that we are co-laborers for the same purpose.

"destined for this" [v. 3]
Being "destined" refers to a person's future happening according to a plan or expected outcome. In this instance, it refers to the fact that as Christians, we are to expect afflictions; they are certain to happen. Thus, we are "destined" for affliction.

"labor in vain" [v. 5]
Paul's concern is that the Tempter may have led them away from faith, undermining the impact of the good news or even diminishing it. He poured his life into the churches he planted, loving them as his own children. His fear, therefore, is not merely about lost effort but about the people they had won for Christ being drawn away by the Tempter.

"supply what is lacking in your trust" [v. 10]
Paul is commending the Thessalonians for their trust in both God and the ministry of him and his companions. He also expresses his desire to see them soon, not as a rebuke, but as a reaffirmation of his commitment to them. If any doubts had arisen within their congregation, his visit would serve to strengthen and encourage them.

"God and Father himself and our Lord Jesus" [v. 11]
One of many examples where Paul clearly distinguishes between God the Father and Jesus as two separate and distinct beings. Recognizing this distinction is crucial as the doctrine of the trinity has been widely accepted from

the Council of Nicaea onward (A.D. 325) stipulates that God the Father and Jesus are the same being. Maintaining this distinction is not only central to Paul's Christology but also foundational to his entire theological framework. This is made clear by Paul making the distinction between the Father and Jesus in the introduction of each of his letters.

STUDY 4

INTRODUCTION

After being concerned about the Thessalonian believers and then receiving the encouraging report from Timothy, Paul now shifts focus to the practical outworking of the Thessalonians's faith. While their love and steadfastness in the good news had become well-known, Paul recognized the importance of continuing to guide them in their daily lives for spiritual growth in following Christ. Thessalonica, a prominent city in Macedonia, was steeped in cultural practices that often conflicted with the Christian call to holiness. Pagan worship, sexual immorality, and a focus on self-indulgence were ingrained in the city's way of life. For these new believers, living in a manner that pleased God required not only a deep, spiritual devotion to God, but also a deliberate turning away from cultural norms.

Paul also reminds the Thessalonians of the instructions they had already received during his brief stay. His words are not new commands but a reinforcement of the call to live in holiness and love. He emphasizes that their conduct matters—not just as a product of their personal faith, but also as a witness to those around them. Paul's approach is pastoral and practical, providing guidance on specific areas like sexual purity, brotherly love, and living a peaceful, productive life.

In doing so, Paul ties their daily actions to their trust in Christ and the message of the good news, showing that every aspect of life should reflect their commitment to God. His message remains deeply relevant today, as believers continue to navigate the tension between cultural pressures and the call to live as God's holy people.

STUDY QUESTIONS

1. Paul strongly urges the Thessalonians to "walk and please God" in their daily lives. What are some practical habits or choices we can make to pursue this in our own lives and be a positive example to others? [1 Thess. 4:2]

2 We learn that God's will is for us to be holy and abstain from sexual immorality. How does this calling to holiness contrast with the values of today's culture? [1 Thess. 4:3]

3 Paul mentions each person is to control their "own vessel in holiness and honor." What cultural issue does he contrast this with? And why is it correlated with not knowing God? [1 Thess 4:4-5]

4 What are the "proper boundaries" that Paul is instructing believers to not overstep? Why do you think he stresses the importance of not "taking advantage" of fellow believers? [1 Thess. 4:6]

5 Holiness can sometimes feel like an overwhelming concept to grasp. How would you describe God's holiness? How does understanding His holiness impact our relationship with Him? [1 Thess. 4:7]

6 Paul makes it clear that these commands come from God, not just from human authority. He warns that rejecting them is rejecting God. Why do you think Paul stresses this point? [1 Thess. 4:8]

7 Relationships within the Body of Christ are unique because they bring together people from different backgrounds and personalities. While some relationships form naturally, others may take more effort. How can we actively nurture "affection for God's family" in our relationships to strengthen unity in the church? [1 Thess. 4:9]

8 Paul notes that the Thessalonians had an impact across all of Macedonia, a region that's over 15,000 square miles. How can you use your resources–your time, connections, location, etc.– to bring Christ to those around you? [1 Thess. 4:10]

9 Paul encourages believers to "lead a peaceable life, and attend to your own business, and work with your hands". What do these verses reveal about the Christian work ethic and lifestyle? How can these principles shape the way we approach our work, relationships, and daily responsibilities? [1 Thess. 4:11-12]

WORD DEFINITIONS

HOLY [v. 3]
Holiness is the concept of being morally distinct from the world and having one's thoughts and behavior aligned with God's will. To be holy is to follow Jesus' example

who did the will of God in every situation. In contrast, unholiness is to conform to the ways of the world which run completely counter to God's will for His people.

SEXUALLY IMMORALITY [v. 3]
Sexual immorality encompasses various sins, including adultery, same-sex relations, lust, pornography, and all forms of sexual abuse and sexually deviant behavior.

VESSEL [v. 4]
A "vessel" refers to a person's body, and in this passage, the phrase "control your own vessel" is a metaphorical way of describing self-control. A person is to have their body under their control like the way a captain controls the direction of a ship ("vessel").

HOLINESS [v. 4]
Holiness is the ongoing pursuit of growing in devotion and obedience to God and turning away from sin. It is a lifelong journey that will be fully perfected when Jesus returns and God's people (i.e., the holy ones) are resurrected to new bodies free from the power of sin and death.

LUSTFUL PASSION [v. 5]
This refers to the desires of one's body to indulge in acts of sexual immorality, which harm themselves and others. These desires are sinful and dishonorable in the eyes of God.

GENTILES [v. 5]
"Gentile" is the term that refers to all non-Jewish individuals (also called "pagans"). In the New Testament, the

Gentiles are often contrasted with the "Jews" as a way to distinguish ethnic differences, but more importantly, religious differences. Gentiles were polytheists who worshipped the pantheon of Greek/Roman gods, while the Jews were monotheists, worshipping Yahweh alone—the God of Israel.

PEACEABLE LIFE [v. 11]

A peaceable life involves pursuing honest work to support oneself and one's family while fostering good relationships both within the church and in the broader community and society.

OUTSIDERS [v. 12]

"Outsiders" refers to those who are not part of the church, and thus is a way to refer to unbelievers. The term "outsiders" is also implicitly covenantal language where an "outsider" is a person who is not part of God's new covenant in Christ.

ADDITIONAL NOTES

"the will of God" [v. 3]

People often seek to understand God's will for their life, as though it entails a particular, defined course or specific path they are to take. Yet Scripture consistently reveals that God's will is for people to live with moral purity and love for others. When we align our lives with this foundational truth, we become more attuned to

God's guidance and help in living in ways that honor and please Him each day.

"the Lord is an avenger" [v. 6]

This phrase highlights God's deep concern for justice and the fair treatment of others, warning against taking advantage of fellow believers (or anyone in general). When wrongdoing occurs, God Himself will bring justice to those who have been wronged. This not only affirms His care for our individual actions but also assures us that He will decisively address such offenses at the judgment in the age to come. Therefore, we need not seek vengeance ourselves, as that action and responsibility belong to God.

"affection for God's family" [v. 9]

Loving fellow believers is an expression of affection for God's family. When we care for one another, we demonstrate love and concern, not just for our spiritual family, but for God's family as a whole, since all who believe are adopted as His children. This highlights the importance of treating one another with mutual kindness and respect.

"walk properly toward outsiders" [v. 12]

Our actions impact not only ourselves and the family of God, but also how the outside world perceives the church, who are to be followers of Christ. When we misrepresent Christ and his values, we harm the kingdom of God rather than advancing it. Walking properly toward outsiders means living in a way that reflects our role as God's representatives and ambassadors of His kingdom.

STUDY 5

INTRODUCTION

In this part of his letter, Paul turns his attention to the return of Jesus and the resurrection of the dead, offering both reassurance and clarity to the Thessalonian believers. The resurrection of Christ is the foundation of the Christian faith, so understanding what it means—and what will happen when Christ returns—is essential to their faith. Paul's detail in this matter suggests that the Thessalonians were troubled about it. Perhaps they feared that their loved ones who had died before Christ's return might somehow miss out on the blessings of His kingdom. Sensing their distress, Paul corrects their misunderstanding, assuring them that those who have died in Christ will actually be raised to life first and will absolutely take part in Christ's glorious return.

Christ's return is pictured as a glorious, triumphal occasion with a heavenly announcement and trumpet blast that will make known to the world the majestic arrival of the Lord Jesus. This grand depiction of the Lord's return is meant to instill in the Thessalonians a sense of comfort and hope regarding this future reality, in which both they and the believers who have died will participate.

Paul also stresses the sudden and unpredictable nature of Jesus' coming. Therefore, believers must remain spiritually awake and prepared because no one knows the exact moment of Christ's return. He paints a vivid contrast: those who live as children of the light—walking in holiness and vigilance—versus those lost in darkness, unaware and unready for what is to come. His message is both urgent and hopeful—live each day in readiness, allowing the promise of Christ's return to shape a life of faithfulness and holiness.

STUDY QUESTIONS

1   Paul concludes chapter 4 with the topics of death, grief, and hope. What circumstances might have prompted Paul to address those topics? [1 Thess. 4:13]

2 What is the difference between grieving with and without hope? How have you seen or experienced these differences in your own life or seen them in others? [1 Thess. 4:13]

3 Paul encourages the believers that because Jesus was raised from the dead, we also believe that he will raise us up from the dead. How does this promise shape your perspective on life and death? In what ways does it influence your hope and faith each day? [1 Thess. 4:14]

4 Jesus' birth was humble and unassuming (i.e., modest and simple). How does this contrast with the triumphant and grand depiction of his return from heaven? [1 Thess. 4:16]

5 What role does community play in encouraging one another with the truth of the resurrection? How can we practically apply this in our relationships and communities? [1 Thess. 4:18]

6 What does Paul mean that Jesus' return will come "like a thief in the night"? What are ways that we can live with readiness for the Lord's return? [1 Thess. 5:2-3]

7 Paul uses "asleep" and "awake," and "darkness" and "light" as contrasting metaphors. What do you think these metaphors signify about spiritual awareness and personal conduct? [1 Thess. 5:5-6]

8 Paul calls believers to be "awake and clear-headed". What are some ways people today fall into spiritual "sleep," and how can we be mindful to fight against that in our own lives? [1 Thess. 5:6-7]

WORD DEFINITIONS

ASLEEP [v. 13]

The Bible often uses the term "sleep" as a euphemism for death, offering insight into biblical theology regarding the state of the dead—an unconscious condition similar to sleep. This metaphor is reinforced by the Greek word *anastasis*, which means "to awaken" or "to arouse," yet it is also used in the New Testament to describe the bodily resurrection that will occur at Christ's return.

COMING OF THE LORD [v. 15]

The coming of the Lord refers repeatedly to Jesus' return at the dawn of the age to come, on the last day of this present age. While Paul does not provide as much detail as some other biblical authors, his depiction of the triumphant Christ remains vivid and awe-inspiring and is therefore the basis of hope and belief not only for Paul but for all of those who receive his message.

RULING ANGEL [v. 16]

A "ruling angel" is a powerful spiritual being who executes God's will and protects God's people in spiritual warfare. The term "ruling angel" is traditionally translated as "archangel" in the Bible. They are high-ranking angels with greater authority than other angels. The only "ruling angel" mentioned explicitly in Scripture is Michael (Jude 1:9; cf. Rev. 12:7). He leads God's heavenly army, defends God's people against evil forces, and plays a key role in end-time events.

IN THE CLOUDS [v. 17]

This is a reference to the physical and literal return of Christ. The angels, in Acts 1, state that Jesus will return in the same manner that he had left - he was assumed into heaven bodily, and he will have a bodily return.

DAY OF THE LORD [5:2]

The day of the Lord is when God brings judgment upon the wicked and grants life to the saints in the age to come. This is also closely related to the "coming of the Lord" in verse 15. Both of these phrases speak of the same event - the day Jesus returns, dispenses justice, and inaugurates his father's kingdom.

ADDITIONAL NOTES

"so that they will be with him" [v. 14]
Although many theologians, for over a millennium, have taught that believers go to heaven to be with Jesus

immediately when they die, this phrase clarifies that believers must be raised from the dead to be with Jesus. Consequently, it implies that we are not with him before the resurrection of our bodies. This reinforces his choice to describe the dead as "asleep."

"suddenly caught up together" [v. 17]

Rather than being a mere escape from the present evil age, the being "caught up together" signifies a sudden unification of believers when the Lord returns—both those who are deceased and then resurrected, and those still living whose bodies will be transformed. The phrase is translated from the Greek word *harpazō*, which refers to seizing, snatching, or grasping something or someone quickly, and often with force. So, the resurrected believers and those who will be transformed into new bodies will be brought together in a sudden and rapid manner for a meeting with the Lord in the air. Theologically, this event is often referred to as the Rapture.

"meeting" [v. 17]

The Greek word *apantēsis* describes a meeting that includes a lavish welcome and greeting, often with much fanfare and honors being demonstrated. In the Roman Empire, citizens of colonies would go out, sometimes many miles away from the city, to meet and welcome high-ranking officials or dignitaries to the city (e.g., the emperor) as they were approaching. Thus, the purpose of gathering together the believers who have been raised from the dead or transformed to have new, glorious bodies is to go up into the air and meet Lord Jesus as one would in the Roman culture for a person of high authority or great renown.

"a thief in the night" [5:2]

This verse highlights the unpredictable nature of Jesus' return. While Scripture provides signs and many have attempted to use them to predict his coming, history shows that such predictions not only cause harm and disillusionment but also foster a sense of eschatological superiority. The beauty of this simple truth is that since we do not know when Jesus will return, we should live in constant readiness, always awaiting his arrival.

"children of light/day" [5:5]

This presents a clear contrast to the children of darkness, using a metaphor to emphasize the distinction between God's children, the children of light, and those who live in disobedience, the children of the night.

STUDY 6

INTRODUCTION

As Paul nears the end of his letter to the Thessalonians, he takes the opportunity to pour out words of encouragement, much like a loving father guiding his children. He urges them to continue walking in a way that honors God, reinforcing their faithfulness and devotion. Utilizing militaristic imagery, Paul paints a picture of the Christian life as a battle and stresses the need to be equipped with spiritual armor—trust, love, and the hope of salvation.

Beyond personal devotion and mutual encouragement in the faith, Paul emphasizes the importance of honoring those who lead in the church, recognizing their role in shepherding the community. He also addresses the issue of seeking revenge for oneself; rather, believers are to seek what is good for everyone. Following that, he then offers a series of practical exhortations, a short but powerful list of instructions for living spiritually mature lives that honor God.

Finally, Paul brings his letter to a close with a heartfelt desire—that the Thessalonians would remain steadfast, unshaken in their faith, until the return of the Lord Jesus. His words serve as both a challenge and a comfort, calling them to perseverance while reminding them of the hope for what is still to come.

STUDY QUESTIONS

1 Believers are called to be "clear-headed" and to put on trust, love, and hope as spiritual armor. How do these metaphors help us understand our spiritual armor, and how we can protect ourselves against the Adversary? [1 Thess. 5:8]

2 How can we actively fulfill Paul's command to "encourage one another" and "build each other up" based on the truth that we are not appointed to God's wrath, but to obtain salvation? [1 Thess. 5:9-11]

3 Paul gives instructions about how to treat leaders in the church. What do these verses teach about the attitude and actions we are to adopt toward those who lead and guide us in the faith? [1 Thess. 5:12-13]

4 Paul encourages the believers to admonish the undisciplined, comfort the discouraged, help the weak, and be patient with everyone. Which of these challenges you the most, and why? How can we apply these principles in our interactions with others, especially when we know they will resist hearing it? [1 Thess. 5:14]

5 Believers are instructed to "diligently pursue what is good." What does it mean to "diligently pursue" something, and what is Paul pointing to when he says to actively seek "what is good"? Why is this endeavor so important for our lives, especially in the face of evil or adversity? [1 Thess. 5:15]

6 Paul uses strong, resolute language—"always," "never," and "in everything". Why do you think he emphasizes these words in relation to joy, prayer, and thanksgiving? [1 Thess. 5:16-18]

7 Paul instructs believers to "test everything" and "hold on firmly" to what is good, while rejecting evil. What does it look like to "test" teachings and prophecies in order to discern between what is good and evil? [1 Thess. 5:21-22]

8 What is revealed about the importance of God's faithfulness in Paul's prayer that the Thessalonians be made "completely holy"? [1 Thess. 5:23-24]

9 Imagine you are a believer in Thessalonica hearing this letter read aloud for the first time. What impression do you get from how Paul closes his letter with his final words? [1 Thess. 5:25-28]

10 After studying 1 Thessalonians, was there a particular verse or theme that challenged or deepened your understanding of God's character or your relationship with Him? How can these insights impact your journey in faith and daily walk with the Lord?

◆

WORD DEFINITIONS

BREASTPLATE OF TRUST AND LOVE [v. 8]
An image that would have deeply resonated with a community living in a Roman province is that of a soldier's breastplate—a piece of armor designed to shield a soldier's most vital organs, protecting the heart, lungs, and core. Paul uses this metaphor to emphasize the necessity of spiritual discipline, just as soldiers are

trained to wear their armor without fail. In the same way, Christians must actively put on the breastplate of faith and love. Without it, we are as vulnerable as a Roman legionnaire entering battle without his armor—exposed to the enemy's attacks. When we neglect trust in God and love for others, we leave ourselves open to the schemes of the Tempter, lacking the protection we desperately need.

HELMET OF THE HOPE OF SALVATION [v. 8]

Another essential piece of the Roman military uniform was the helmet, designed to protect not only the brain but also, to some degree, the eyes—safeguarding both thought and vision. In the same way, Paul's imagery reminds us that if we do not continually fill our minds with the truth of God's salvation, we leave ourselves vulnerable to the enemy's attacks. Just as a soldier without a helmet is exposed to fatal blows, so too is a believer whose mind is unguarded. And once the head is taken, the battle is lost.

QUENCH THE SPIRIT [v. 19]

This phrase clearly demonstrates that God's grace is not irresistible; rather, we must actively ensure that we do not hinder the Spirit's work in our lives. How do we quench the Spirit? By ignoring God's promptings, conforming to the sinful ways of the world, and resisting His truth through unrepentance.

HOLY [v. 23]

To be holy means for us to be set apart and distinct from the world. God is holy, meaning He is completely separate from sin, evil, and wickedness. For us, holiness means becoming more like God and less like the world. Conversely, unholiness is conforming to the world and living in a way that reflects less of God.

HOLY KISS [v. 26]

A customary greeting in the Ancient Near East was a kiss, a gesture of love and affection. This practice was not meant to be misinterpreted or perverted but instead reflected the deep sense of community that characterized both Ancient Near Eastern and Mediterranean cultures. For the early Christians, this greeting took on even greater significance, symbolizing the close-knit bond of believers united in faith and brotherly love.

ADDITIONAL NOTES

"appoint us to wrath" [v. 9]

This phrase shows that God has not appointed the church as a whole to receive wrath but to be saved from the coming wrath. This appointment applies generally to those who come to saving faith in Jesus Christ within the church, rather than to specific individuals.

"live together with him" [v. 10]

This refers to the final state in which humanity will dwell with the Lord Jesus on the earth. His return is necessary to resurrect the saints to immortality and glorify those still alive at his coming. As Paul explained in chapter 4, when Jesus returns, we will meet him in the air, not to be taken away, but to escort him in a royal welcome as he establishes his reign. From that moment on, we will always live together with him.

"hold them in very high regard" [v. 13]

This verse emphasizes the importance of holding church leadership in high regard. While church leaders are not infallible, they should be valued, loved, and appreciated, as they are given for our good as shepherds of the church and caretakers of our souls.

"test everything" [v. 21]

Testing everything refers to evaluating prophecies shared by other Christians. This doesn't mean being overly critical, but rather seeking discernment to determine whether a message is truly from God. This testing involves praying for spiritual insight and comparing the message to Scripture, as God will not contradict Himself.

"your whole spirit and soul and body" [v. 23]

Human beings are composed of a tripartite ("triple part") nature that consists of: a body, soul, and spirit. Each of these elements is essential for human existence; without any one of them, it would not constitute a human being. Paul is not exactly clear on what distinction he is making between "soul" and "spirit," but he apparently finds something to differentiate the human "spirit" (which is used to refer to the mind of a person), and the human "soul" (which is used to refer to the animating [i.e., life-sustaining] force in a person). Whatever distinction Paul is making, his focus is on the Thessalonians' sanctification (i.e., being holy). Thus, Paul invokes this understanding of human existence to emphasize in his prayer for the Thessalonians that he has the entirety of their being—body, soul, and spirit—in his mind when he asks that God would preserve them blameless until the coming of the Lord Jesus.

2 THESSALONIANS INTRODUCTION

Second Thessalonians is an ancient letter written by the apostle Paul together with his companions Silvanus and Timothy (1:1), addressed again to the congregations in Thessalonica. It follows rather closely the heart of 1 Thessalonians and carries Paul's pastoral mission forward: to steady the believers amid persecution and to clarify confusion about the return of the Lord. To begin, Paul thanks God for their growing trust and love (1:3) and boasts to other churches about their endurance and faith in "all the persecutions and afflictions" they are bearing (1:4). He assures them that their steadfastness is evidence of God's righteous judgment and assures them that God's justice will be served when the Lord Jesus returns (1:5-10). His prayer is that they would reflect the message of the good news in their life and thereby be counted worthy of their calling (1:11-12).

A central purpose of the letter is to correct the false notion and alarm in the church that "the day of the Lord" had already come (2:1-2). Such an idea would have caused great unrest and distress among the congregations. Therefore, Paul urges them not to be quickly shaken—whether by a spirit, a message, or a letter supposedly from the apostles. Before that day arrives, Paul declares that certain events must take place: 1) a great rebellion will occur, and 2) "the man of lawlessness," who opposes God and exalts himself, will be revealed (2:3-4). The identity of this figure is not revealed, but Paul reassures the Thessalonians that this person is presently restrained, but the restraint will be removed in God's timing. But this lawless one will be made known and then ultimately destroyed at the Lord's appearing (2:6-8). And to this end, Paul warns them of the deceptive power, signs, and wonders that will test those who refuse the love of the truth (2:9-12). Against such turmoil and adversity, he charges the Thessalonians to "stand firm and hold to the traditions" delivered to them—whether spoken or written by the apostles (2:15).

Attention is then turned toward practical concerns in the church with Paul praying that the word of the Lord will spread rapidly and be honored, and that the workers of the good news be rescued from unreasonable and evil people as they serve God's kingdom (3:1-2). But the Thessalonian churches are not without their issues as Paul moves to address disorderliness within the community, especially idleness, stipulating that the community is to keep away from any believer who refuses to live according to apostolic teaching and example (3:6). This example was demonstrated firsthand by Paul himself when he was with the Thessalonians (3:7-9). So adamant is Paul about this that he reiterates the rule: "If anyone is not willing to work, neither let him eat" (3:10). Yet even in this course of discipline, Paul's tone remains pastoral as he admonishes them not to regard the disobedient as enemies, but rather to warn them as brothers and sisters in Christ (3:14-15). The letter closes with one of Paul's typical benedictions of peace and grace from the Lord Jesus (3:16-18), encapsulating his overall aim in the letter: to anchor the Thessalonians in hope, holiness, and steadfastness until Christ's return.

STUDY 7

INTRODUCTION

Paul opens his second letter addressing the Thessalonian communities with the same warm, fatherly, and pastoral tone he used in his first letter. He rejoices not because they have been spared hardship, but because they have remained faithful followers of Christ amid ongoing trials. The theme of hardship is neither new nor unique to this letter—it is a well-established part of Paul's encouragement and exhortation to the Thessalonian congregations. Despite their challenges, the Thessalonians displayed remarkable trust in God and steadfast endurance as they continued spreading the message of the kingdom of God. Rather than being hindered by persecution, the good news about Jesus advanced and flourished amid the early church's suffering.

Paul reassures them that their suffering for the sake of God's kingdom has not gone unnoticed by God. He affirms that God sees their affliction and will one day set things right. Paul clarifies that justice for the wrongs they have endured will come—not arbitrarily, but at the proper time—when Jesus returns. As a source of encouragement, he points to that great day when the Lord Jesus will appear, reminding them that God has called His people to proclaim the good news until that day comes. Paul also assures them of his regular prayers that the Thessalonians continue glorifying the name of the Lord Jesus in both their ministry and daily lives. In this opening chapter, Paul demonstrates that sound doctrine is not just for instruction but also for equipping and encouraging fellow believers to live out the kingdom message.

STUDY QUESTIONS

1 How can we nurture a growing trust in God and love for our fellow believers? [2 Thess. 1:3]

2 What are some visible signs that our trust in God is increasing in our lives? [2 Thess. 1:3]

3 What are some temptations that can affect our trust in God when we are going through hardships or afflictions? [2 Thess. 1:4]

4 Why is endurance and trusting God so important when going through trials? [2 Thess. 1:4]

5 What is the relationship between suffering for the kingdom of God and being found worthy of it? [2 Thess. 1:5]

6 How does the promise that God will bring justice to those who wrong us impact the way we respond when we are wronged? [2 Thess. 1:6]

7 Why do you think Paul uses such vivid warrior imagery to describe Jesus at his return, and how should that shape our view of him? [2 Thess. 1:7]

8 Why does Paul mention the punishment of those who oppose the good news? Why is it important to understand what "eternal destruction" and "separation" from God mean? [2 Thess. 1:8-9]

9 Paul highlights the importance of having godly motivation and desire for moral goodness in life. What can we do to help our motivations and desires be more aligned with God's will? [2 Thess. 1:11-12]

---◇---

WORD DEFINITIONS

HEAVEN [v. 7]
Heaven has a wide range of uses in the Bible. It commonly refers to the sky where birds fly, outer space, or the realm where God dwells. In this passage, it refers specifically to the spiritual realm where God and the Lord Jesus currently reside.

FLAMING FIRE [v. 8]
Fire, metaphorically, refers to the power of Christ's judgment that will consume and destroy God's enemies. When Christ returns, he will cleanse the earth of wickedness and establish the reign of righteousness.

THAT DAY [v. 10]
This refers to the end of the present evil age. The Old Testament often calls it the Day of the Lord, and according to the New Testament writers, this is the day of Christ's return, the resurrection, and God's judgment.

HOLY ONES [v. 10]

To be "holy" refers to the act of setting oneself apart from the world, in accordance with God's will for humanity. The phrase "holy ones" is commonly translated as "saints" and is a designation for all born-again believers. This identity as "holy ones" is a present reality for all believers, not a title bestowed after one's death. Furthermore, the presence of God's holy spirit inside of believers is what sets them apart as "holy ones."

ADDITIONAL NOTES

"kingdom of God" [v. 5]

The kingdom of God is the culmination of all of God's plans and promises at the end of the age—everlasting life, eternal peace, and unending fellowship with both God our Father and His Son Jesus Christ. The New Testament authors also understand God's kingdom as something already present in the world but not yet fully realized. There is a future time where God's kingdom will come in its complete fullness.

"judgment of God" [v. 5]

The judgment of God is something that occurs partially in the present, and has also occurred throughout all of history. However, the primary meaning of God's judgment in both the Old and New Testaments is a future event that will take place in the age to come when God will punish evildoers according to His justice and cleanse all evil and wickedness from the earth. This event is closely associated with the return of the Lord Jesus and the realities of the age to come.

"everlasting destruction" [v. 9]

The Greek word *aiōnios*, often translated as "everlasting," can be understood either in terms of duration or as a permanent and irreversible action. The New and Old Testaments agree that those who do not partake in God's kingdom will not experience ongoing punishment forever but will be destroyed. This everlasting destruction should be understood qualitatively, referring to the definiteness and totality of the destruction, not with respect to a duration of time.

STUDY 8

INTRODUCTION

After beginning the letter with such encouragement during persecution, Paul takes a sharp turn in the letter in chapter 2. Not only does the apostle Paul use language that has left many readers scratching their heads, but he also gives us a glimpse into his unique knowledge of the end times. Paul reminds the Thessalonians that he had already spoken about these things in person, but makes a brief mention here of them. This section also contains the only mention of the phrase "the man of lawlessness," making the passage complex and unique.

The key theme of the section is focused on the end times. Paul addresses a deception that was spreading about how some were saying the end times were already taking place—or more specifically, that the "Day of the Lord," the cataclysmic battle at the end of the age, had already come. Some were teaching that the return of Jesus had already occurred in secret. Paul was concerned that the Thessalonians would hear and believe these false doctrines. His tone is quite emphatic: he does not want them to be swept away by such deceivers into believing a lie.

He also warns that this "man of lawlessness" will come with impressive signs and powers, but he is not empowered by God, for they are, in fact, the work of the Adversary. Paul includes this warning because people who are unaware of the coming of this lawless one might be deceived by the false signs and miracles that he will do. Nevertheless, Paul is confident in the Thessalonians and wants to make sure they continue to stand firm on the truth.

STUDY QUESTIONS

1 Why is it important to understand the future promise of the Lord's coming? [2 Thess. 2:1-2]

2 Paul cautions the Thessalonians not to be deceived. Without exclusively talking about specific doctrines, what are some examples of false ideas that Christians can fall into believing? [2 Thess. 2:3]

3 What does "the sanctuary of God" refer to where Paul says the man of lawlessness will set himself up as a god? [2 Thess. 2:3-5]

4 The coming of the man of lawlessness is currently being prevented. But once he is revealed, Jesus will destroy him at his return. What is the significance of the coming of the man of lawlessness in the end times? (cf. vv. 3-4) [2 Thess. 2:6-8]

5 If the Adversary will perform counterfeit miracles through the lawless one, how do we as Christians discern the difference between a counterfeit miracle and the genuine working of God? [2 Thess. 2:9]

6 If deception comes as a result of rejecting the good news, what does that imply about our role in proclaiming and discipling others in the message of Christ? [2 Thess. 2:10]

7 God allows people to follow the paths they choose, even when those paths lead them away from truth—and there are real consequences for that. How can we gently and lovingly encourage fellow believers to continue to walk in the truth and not drift into error? [2 Thess. 2:11-12]

8 What are some practical ways that we can be prepared for the Day of the Lord, whether it comes during our lifetime or not?

WORD DEFINITIONS

APOSTASY [v. 3]

The act of apostasy is falling away from the Christian faith. It is a deliberate rejection and opposition to God, the Lord Jesus, and the message of the good news. While there are many who have departed and renounced their faith throughout history, in the end times, there will be a mass apostasy—a great falling away from the faith.

MAN OF LAWLESSNESS [v. 3]

A man of lawlessness is one who purposefully disregards the statutes and expectations of God and is therefore under no law. Although many people can be lawless persons, it is clear that there is a chief man of lawlessness in the future. See the additional note.

EXALTS [v. 4]

To exalt something is to raise something in praise or adoration in your heart. When we sing songs of praise or talk about the goodness of God, we are exalting Him. When he comes, the man of lawlessness will wrongfully exalt himself, striving to be worshipped in God's place.

SO-CALLED "GOD" [v. 4]

This refers to the false idols and deities promoted by pagan cultures, in contrast to the true God, who is exalted above and superior to every idol and object of worship in the world.

COUNTERFEIT SIGNS AND WONDERS [v. 9]

Refers to the miracles and demonstrations of power that are performed through the man of lawlessness by the working of Satan. These false signs will mislead many into believing the man of lawlessness rather than recognizing his true role as a deceiver.

ADDITIONAL NOTES

"spirit-inspired utterance" [v. 2]

A spirit-inspired utterance is not to be confused with the genuine, inspired utterance through the power of God's holy spirit. In this context, it refers to the work of a wicked spirit that seeks to deceive by wrongly alarming believers about the timing of the day of the Lord. This is a serious pitfall with real consequences—believers must remain vigilant against the work of all evil spirits.

"Day of the Lord" [v. 2]

This refers to the day when Jesus returns to carry out judgment against all wickedness, preparing the way for God's return to be with His creation. This time includes a cataclysmic battle in which Jesus defeats evil, vanquishing and destroying the adversary forever.

"man of lawlessness" [v. 3]

Theologians have debated for centuries who the man of lawlessness is. Borrowing language from the epistles of John, he appears to be an end-times Antichrist-type figure who leads a great apostasy, drawing many away from the faith at the end of the age. His doom, however, is ensured, as his influence will be brought to an end at the coming of Jesus. And a simple "word" (i.e., spirit) from the mouth of Jesus is enough to completely destroy him.

"spirit from his mouth" [v. 8]

Jesus' power is contrasted with the work of the lawless one, whom Jesus destroys with the utterance of his mouth. The "spirit" that comes from his mouth is a spirit-inspired utterance that carries power with it. The phrase can also be translated as "breath from his mouth," which might be a metonymy for the words that he will speak, or a metaphor for the power of his judgment poured out upon his enemies. This not only reveals the vast difference in power between Jesus and the man of lawlessness, but also demonstrates that the victory will be swift and final.

STUDY 9

INTRODUCTION

After outlining the dangers of deception and the coming of the "man of lawlessness," Paul turns to conveying his reassurance and encouragement. He reminds the Thessalonian believers that they are dearly loved by the Lord and chosen as "firstfruits for salvation," emphasizing their special place in God's redemptive plan. He further highlights that their salvation is accomplished through the sanctifying work of the spirit and their reliance upon the truth, underscoring both God's initiative and their response in faith.

Paul's encouragement also includes an exhortation for the Thessalonians not to depart from the "traditions" passed down by him and the other apostles. In other early Christian communities, the devastation that results when believers stray from sound teaching and follow those who teach falsely—whether intentionally or unintentionally—is evident in some of Paul's other letters. Thus, Paul's hope for the Thessalonians is that they would be continually strengthened to live out good works and stand firm in sound doctrine. All of this flows from God's grace, which is the foundation of their hope in God's kingdom.

At the beginning of chapter 3, Paul requests prayer from the Thessalonians and expresses a sense of urgency about spreading the "word of the Lord"—a phrase he often uses as shorthand for the good news of the cross, resurrection, and the kingdom of God. After offering further encouragement about the faithfulness of the Lord and his protection, Paul again exhorts them to endure in the Lord, who has directed their hearts toward love, and declares his full confidence that the Thessalonian believers will continue to live this out as their aim and calling.

STUDY QUESTIONS

1 Paul states that salvation comes through holiness produced by the spirit and believing the truth. Seeing that holiness is vitally important, how do we pursue holiness as Christians? [2 Thess. 2:13-14]

2 What role should tradition play within Christian beliefs, and how might it help us stand firm in the truth? [2 Thess. 2:15]

3 The Thessalonians, along with other first-century churches, faced much persecution. What might God be strengthening and guarding our hearts against today, even if we do not experience the same persecution? [2 Thess. 2:16-17]

4 Paul asks the Thessalonians to pray for him and his companions, for their continued ministry, and for the removal of any opposition against them. What can we pray for today that reflects the heart of Paul's prayer? [2 Thess. 3:1-2]

5   Paul prays for the good news to spread quickly and to be glorified. How can we fulfill Paul's prayer to honor and hasten the spread of the good news in our local community? [2 Thess. 3:1]

6   The faithfulness of the Lord is what guards us from the Wicked One—the Adversary. What schemes do you see the Adversary working against believers today? [2 Thess. 3:3]

7   How should Christians encourage and challenge each other to live out the commands of God from both the Apostles and the Scriptures? [2 Thess. 3:4]

8 Paul was confident in the Thessalonians' obedience and faithfulness to following the commands of the apostles. Why does he then pray that God would guide their hearts into love and endurance? [2 Thess. 3:4-5]

9 Take a moment to reflect on the people in your life. Who has God placed in your life to pray for this week, that they would experience His love more deeply? [2 Thess. 3:5]

— ◇ —

WORD DEFINITIONS

FIRSTFRUITS [v. 13]
This phrase is used in Scripture to indicate something that is first in order or significance. In the biblical culture, farmers would take the first portion of their harvest and

offer it to God. This was a way to honor God and recognize that the fruit of the harvest came from Him.

WICKED ONE [3:3]

This is a reference to the spiritual adversary of both God and believers that is often referred to as "Satan" or the "Devil." The adversary seeks to harm Christians and hinder the advancement of the good news about God's kingdom and His Messiah.

ADDITIONAL NOTES

"firstfruits" [v. 13]

While the Thessalonians were not the first group of Gentiles to believe, they will be part of the "firstfruits" of salvation when the Lord Jesus returns. Furthermore, Jesus himself is referred to as the firstfruits of the resurrection since he was the first person raised to new life, never to die again (1 Cor. 15:20-23). And so, the Thessalonians are called the "firstfruits" for salvation because they will be part of the first group who will receive the complete realization of the promised life and blessings in the age to come. However, there is a textual discrepancy in v. 13 that centers on whether the original Greek text used the word "firstfruits" (*aparchē*) or the phrase "from the beginning" (*ap' archē*). The textual decision is difficult as the same Greek letters are used in both readings, and each reading contains theological merit and validity.

"obtain glory" [v. 14]

In the New Testament, glorification for believers—or obtaining glory—is synonymous with receiving a resurrection body. When Jesus returns, he will raise believers from the dead, and they will receive imperishable bodies: new, glorious bodies.

"traditions you were taught" [v. 15]

Paul is referring to the doctrines and teachings that came directly from the apostles. In the first century, false teachers were leading others astray, and some of Paul's congregations—such as the Galatians—had been affected by their efforts. Holding fast to the apostolic traditions and teachings was the most reliable way to remain grounded in the truth.

"harmful and wicked people" [3:2]

These are people who were opposing the good news. However, this isn't limited to one particular group; it includes all who stand against Jesus and the spread of his kingdom message. For Paul, this opposition often came from both Jews and Gentiles alike.

"endurance of Christ" [3:5]

During his earthly ministry, Jesus demonstrated the epitome of endurance. He never gave up or relented, even when faced with a brutal and humiliating public execution. To pray for the "endurance of Christ" is to ask for a strength beyond ourselves—a strength that enables us to remain faithful to God no matter what.

STUDY 10

INTRODUCTION

In the closing section of his letter, Paul shifts the focus from eschatological concerns to practical issues within the Thessalonian community. From the position of his apostolic authority, he commands the believers to keep away from believers who live in idleness and do not follow the tradition they received from Paul and his companions. Paul emphasizes the responsibility of each member to contribute to the community's work. Alongside this warning, he also speaks against laziness, bluntly stating that those who are unwilling to work should not eat. This is not a condemnation of those who are unable to work, but of those who are able and choose not to participate in productive and honest labor.

One of the key issues Paul addresses is the problem of idleness—some in the community were refusing to work, perhaps thinking the Lord's return was imminent. But Paul makes it clear that no one in the church should be a burden to others. To that end, he points to his own example,

reminding them that when he visited, he supported himself and even paid for his own food. Therefore, he encourages them not to grow weary in doing good but to persevere in their efforts. He also warns against those who reject apostolic authority and seek to follow their own desires. Above all else, Paul desires unity and urges all believers to conduct themselves in a way that honors both God and the message of the good news. In closing, he specifically draws attention to the letter's authenticity by writing a farewell greeting in his own hand, thus indicating it as genuinely coming from him.

STUDY QUESTIONS

1 Why does Paul warn the Thessalonians so strongly not to associate with those who departed from the apostolic tradition? [2 Thess. 3:6]

2 What is the importance of being orderly with other believers? How can disorderliness negatively affect our congregations? [2 Thess. 3:6-7, 11]

3 Paul recalls the occasions in which he visited the believers in person. What are the benefits that you personally receive when meeting with other believers, whether in person or online? [2 Thess. 3:7-9]

4 Paul commands that those unwilling to work should not be permitted to eat. Why does Paul emphasize this point in such a stark manner? [2 Thess. 3:10]

5 What's the difference between a "busybody" and someone who is busy accomplishing their work? [2 Thess. 3:11]

6 What is the importance of people individually minding their affairs and providing for themselves? What happens to the church when it's filled with people not thinking this way? [2 Thess. 3:12]

7 Why is Paul concerned with the Thessalonians growing weary in doing good? Is this a concern for modern believers as well? [2 Thess. 3:13]

8 Paul tells the Thessalonians not to associate with those who disregard his instruction and apostolic authority. How can we admonish others to return to obeying the teachings of Christ and the apostles when they have wandered away from them? [2 Thess. 3:14-15]

9 Paul signs the letter with a recognizable mark to verify its authenticity. What potential dangers might arise if an early church were to receive and follow a forged letter claiming to be from Paul? [2 Thess. 3:17]

10 What impacted you personally the most from reading and studying 2 Thessalonians?

WORD DEFINITIONS

BUSYBODIES [v. 11]
The term "busybody" reflects someone who appears active but isn't accomplishing anything truly meaningful.

EXHORT [v. 12]
Exhortation is a form of encouragement that carries the weight of a command.

ADMONISH [v. 15]
Admonishment is a form of encouragement that also has the air of correction around it. It is a call to change behavior in order that we are living faithful lives to the Lord and living up to the commands of scripture.

ADDITIONAL NOTES

"walks disorderly" [vv. 6, 11]
The Greek conveys the meaning "to walk out of rank, irregular, or disordered," and is often used in a military context. While the context of this passage clearly links this disorderliness to idleness and refusal to work (vv. 10-11), it can also refer to a broader pattern of undisciplined, irresponsible conduct that includes idleness/laziness.

"we labored and struggled" [v. 8]
The work of the good news was Paul's foremost priority; however, he maintained a bivocational role that allowed him to remain largely self-sufficient during his ministry

journeys. He worked as a tentmaker—a profitable trade in the first century, as temporary shelter was essential for the health and safety of travelers.

"not because we do not have the right to be supported" [v. 9]

Paul uses this phrase to demonstrate that the work of the apostles was worthy of support from the congregations he established, yet he chooses not to accept that support for the benefit of the church and its members. In doing so, Paul sets an example of self-sufficiency that he expects from the believers in Asia Minor.

"busybodies" [v. 11]

The Greek conveys the meaning "working around," in the sense of "busying oneself with trifling matters" or "bustling about needlessly or uselessly." Such people tend to involve themselves in matters that are not their own, and so it is often translated as a "meddler" or "gossiper" in some English versions. Paul uses this word to suggest that people who refuse to work are spending their free time sticking their noses into the business of others, spreading hearsay and rumors, and causing trouble. Thus, a busybody fails to attend to their own responsibilities and instead has an unhealthy interest in interfering with the affairs of others.

"sign of genuineness" [v. 17]

Paul used a personal insignia that would be recognizable to the Thessalonians as his own. It was imperative that they knew the letter they received was truly from Paul and not from someone seeking to harm the church or spread misinformation within his congregations.

RESOURCES FOR FURTHER STUDY

INTRODUCTORY

Wright, N. T. *Paul for Everyone: Galatians and Thessalonians.* Louisville: Westminster John Knox Press, 2004.

Stott, John R. W. *The Message of Thessalonians: The Gospel & the End of Time.* The Bible Speaks Today. Downers Grove, IL: InterVarsity Press, 1991.

Wiersbe, Warren W. *Be Ready: Living in Light of Christ's Return (1 & 2 Thessalonians).* BE Series. Colorado Springs: David C. Cook, 2009.

INTERMEDIATE

Morris, Leon. *The Epistles of Paul to the Thessalonians: An Introduction and Commentary.* Tyndale New Testament Commentaries. Leicester, UK: IVP Academic, 1984.

Bruce, F. F. *1 & 2 Thessalonians.* Word Biblical Themes. Waco, TX: Word Books, 1982.

Green, Gene L. *The Letters to the Thessalonians.* The Pillar New Testament Commentary. Grand Rapids: Eerdmans, 2002.

Holmes, Michael W. *1 and 2 Thessalonians*. The NIV Application Commentary. Grand Rapids: Zondervan, 1998.

ADVANCED

Weima, Jeffrey A. D. *1–2 Thessalonians*. Baker Exegetical Commentary on the New Testament. Grand Rapids: Baker Academic, 2014.

Malherbe, Abraham J. *The Letters to the Thessalonians: A New Translation with Introduction and Commentary*. Anchor Yale Bible Commentary. New Haven: Yale University Press, 2000.

Wanamaker, Charles A. *The Epistles to the Thessalonians: A Commentary on the Greek Text*. New International Greek Testament Commentary. Grand Rapids: Eerdmans, 2013.

ABOUT THE AUTHORS

Pastor Nathan Massie holds a B.A. in Theological Studies from Atlanta Bible College and is currently pursuing a Master of Arts in Theological Studies (M.A.T.S.) at Bethel Seminary in St. Paul, Minnesota, through its remote program. He has served at the Oregon Church of God for five years, where he teaches Adult Sunday School, preaches regularly, and participates in pastoral care. Nathan and his wife, Sarah, live in Oregon, Illinois, with their two cats, Oliver and Poppy. They are grateful to be part of a loving church community and the Church of God General Conference.

Katelyn Salyers earned an Associate's Degree in Theology and Ministry from Atlanta Bible College and is passionate about equipping others to know and love Scripture. She and her husband serve a church community in Tempe, Arizona, where they live with their son. On a typical Sunday, Katelyn can be found playing bass on the worship team or photographing the life of the church. In her free time, she enjoys reading with a coffee in hand, hiking the desert landscape, and spending time with friends.

The Revised English Version (REV) Bible is a modern, committee-based translation published by Spirit & Truth Fellowship International that utilizes an "optimal equivalency" approach that seeks to be faithful to the original languages while ensuring clarity and readability in contemporary English. The stated goal of the translators is to be faithful to the text regardless of traditional readings, which often allows for important biblical truths to be made more clear in the translation.

The REV is distinct in its translation to emphasize specific theological points, such as Yahweh as the one true God, Jesus Christ as Yahweh's only begotten Son and the human Messiah, the importance of human free will, the mortality of the human soul, and the gift of holy spirit in born-again believers. A significant feature of the REV is the extensive, associated commentary that provides explanation and context for many difficult passages. The translation is available for free online at revbible.com and through mobile apps for both iOS and Android.

Scan the QR code to download the mobile app!